Heartbeats in Harmony

In the quiet night, we lay,
Whispers of love begin to sway.
Every heartbeat, a soothing sound,
In your arms, true peace is found.

Stars above twinkle bright,
Guiding our hearts, pure delight.
With every breath, we intertwine,
Two souls blending, so divine.

Moments shared, a gentle sigh,
We rise and fall, like waves nearby.
In this rhythm, we are free,
Just you and I, eternity.

A silent song, our spirits soar,
In the dance of love, we want more.
Fingers trace on skin so warm,
Together weather every storm.

In heartbeats, we find our way,
A harmony that will not fray.
As lovers and friends, we stand strong,
In this bond, we both belong.

Rich Shades of Togetherness

In the morning light, you shine,
A palette of colors, divine.
With every laugh and shared glance,
Life becomes our sweet romance.

Through every season, hand in hand,
We paint our dreams, a vibrant land.
Rich hues of joy, and shades of pain,
Together we dance, forever remain.

The canvas of life, so profound,
In each brushstroke, love is found.
With moments cherished, memories made,
In rich shades, our love won't fade.

By your side, I find my peace,
In your embrace, my heart will cease.
A tapestry of moments great,
In every thread, we celebrate.

Our colors blend, a beautiful sight,
In togetherness, we find our light.
With every heartbeat less apart,
We paint our world, our work of art.

The Dance of Adoration

Underneath the silver moon,
We sway together, a tender tune.
With each step, our spirits glide,
In this dance, love can't hide.

Eyes locked tight, a whispered flame,
Two bodies move, the same old game.
In every twirl, our hearts align,
A rhythm so sweet, beautifully fine.

Hands entwined, the world fades away,
In this moment, we long to stay.
Every glance, a promise made,
In the dance of love, we are unafraid.

With every beat, the night ignites,
Stars bear witness to our flights.
In perfect harmony, we sway and spin,
The dance of adoration, where love begins.

As night turns to dawn, we hold tight,
In this dance, our souls take flight.
Forever together, we take our stand,
In the dance of love, heart in hand.

Iris of the Soul

Deep within, a garden grows,
Blossoms vibrant, love it sows.
In every petal, stories dwell,
An iris blooms, casting its spell.

Colors rich, a vivid hue,
Reflecting all, the me and you.
In the light, your grace unfolds,
With every breath, the heart consoled.

Fragrance sweet, it fills the air,
A bond so strong, beyond compare.
In this garden, time stands still,
The iris of love, an endless thrill.

Through storms and sun, we bravely tread,
With roots entwined, our fears are shed.
In each moment, the soul takes flight,
We blossom forth, a pure delight.

In the iris, our story thrives,
In every heartbeat, love survives.
Together we'll bloom, forever whole,
You are the iris of my soul.

Hues of Happiness

Colors dance in gentle light,
Joyous whispers take their flight.
Every shade, a sweet embrace,
Painting smiles upon each face.

Golden rays of morning sun,
Laughter shared, two hearts as one.
In this canvas, bright and clear,
Happiness is always near.

Azure skies and fields of green,
Nature's beauty, pure and keen.
Each moment, vibrant and true,
Crafting dreams, anew for you.

Crimson sunsets, fiery glow,
Memories in ebb and flow.
With every brushstroke, we find,
Hues of love that bind our minds.

Spectrum of Togetherness

Under the wide, endless skies,
We find our truth as love unties.
Every shade, a story told,
Together brave, together bold.

Rainbows arch with every tear,
Colors bloom, dispelling fear.
Hands united, strong and free,
In this spectrum, you and me.

Brightest hues of trust and care,
In our hearts, dreams brightly flare.
Through each challenge, we will stand,
A spectrum woven, hand in hand.

In laughter shared and pain expressed,
In every moment, we are blessed.
This vibrant thread, a tapestry,
Together sewn eternally.

Colorful Echoes

In the garden where shadows play,
Colors dance in bright array.
Echoes of laughter fill the air,
Whispers of joy are everywhere.

Petals flutter, soft and sweet,
Every hue a rhythmic beat.
Sunlight filters through the trees,
Painting dreams upon the breeze.

Oh, the world in vibrant tone,
Every shade a story known.
From dawn's blush to twilight's grace,
Echoes of life in every space.

Moments shimmer, fleeting spells,
In this realm, the heart compels.
Embrace the colors, let them flow,
In every echo, love will grow.

Vivid Whispers

Beneath the stars that softly gleam,
Whispers rise like a waking dream.
Voices carried on the night,
In their tones, the world feels right.

Every secret, every sigh,
A tapestry of the sky.
Vivid tales in shadows woven,
Promises of paths unchosen.

Through the silence, stories weave,
In the whispers, hearts believe.
Moments shared, a silent call,
In vivid echoes, we rise and fall.

Leave behind the noise of day,
In this hush, our souls shall stay.
Every word, a gentle grace,
In vivid whispers, find our place.

Palette of Promises

In a world where colors blend,
A palette of promises extends.
Brush strokes of hope align,
Creation born from a heart divine.

Every shade a journey's start,
Colors filled with longing heart.
From deep reds to softest blue,
A canvas tells of dreams anew.

Life's brush dances, swift and free,
Painting futures yet to see.
In every hue a tale unfolds,
Whispers of love in tones of gold.

As colors shift, the vision grows,
In this palette, our spirit flows.
Bound by dreams, we begin to soar,
In the artist's hand, we open the door.

Illuminated Intimacy

In the glow of evening's light,
Intimacy feels just right.
Softly spoken, hearts reveal,
Moments shared, emotions real.

Candles flicker, shadows play,
In this warmth, we wish to stay.
Every glance a silent prayer,
In illuminated space, we share.

Secrets linger in the glow,
In this light, our spirits flow.
Every word a gentle touch,
Illuminated, we share so much.

Wrapped in warmth, we find our way,
In this calm, we'll always stay.
In intimacy, our hearts embrace,
In the light, we find our place.

The Flare of Yearning

In the night, a whisper calls,
Echoing through the shadowed halls.
A flicker bright, a spark of hope,
Guiding souls on a fragile rope.

Hearts beat fast in the quiet dark,
Each longing glance, a hidden spark.
Across the void, desires roam,
A distant star, a beckoning home.

Embers dance in the cool night air,
With every sigh, the silent prayer.
A flame ignites with the dawn's first light,
Chasing shadows, embracing the flight.

Lost in dreams, we search for kin,
Through the haze, let the journey begin.
With every breath, we find our way,
In the flare of yearning, we'll stay.

Gentle Strokes of Trust

Softly glows the morning sun,
Trust is built, not just begun.
With every brush, a story flows,
In gentle strokes, the heart just knows.

Fingers trace where words might fail,
In the silence, trust prevails.
Moments shared, both small and grand,
In the tender weave, we understand.

Layers blend in hues of grace,
Finding solace in this space.
A canvas crafted, bold yet kind,
In gentle strokes, true hearts aligned.

Time unfurls like a fragile flower,
Revealing strength in every hour.
With every shift, our spirits dance,
In the embrace of sweet expanse.

Secrets in Subtle Hues

Whispers float on the evening breeze,
Secrets hidden among the trees.
In twilight's glow, colors combine,
Soft revelations, a gentle sign.

Shadows linger, tales untold,
In shades of mystery, we behold.
Every glance, a shade of truth,
In painted worlds, reflecting youth.

The heart knows well what words can't say,
In quiet moments that lead the way.
A palette rich with dreams and fears,
In subtle hues, it draws us near.

Brushstrokes dance in the fading light,
Illuminating the tender night.
Within the silence, stories flow,
In secrets held, love's light will grow.

The Canvas of Memories

Brush and palette, time stands still,
Each stroke captures the heart's great thrill.
Colors flash in vibrant waves,
Moments cherished, the mind saves.

Layers of joy, tinged with pain,
In every hue, the love remains.
Together we painted life so bright,
In the canvas of memories, our light.

Fleeting days, like clouds that drift,
In every shadow, we find our gift.
Holding fast to what makes us whole,
Each memory, a part of the soul.

Captured laughter, whispered dreams,
In the gallery of what love means.
With every glance, a timeless song,
In the canvas of memories, we belong.

Symphony of Vibrant Hearts

In the garden of laughter, we dance,
With colors that weave a bright romance.
Every whisper of joy, every sigh,
A melody sparked, reaching the sky.

Together we sing, hands intertwined,
In rhythm and harmony, souls aligned.
Underneath the stars, our dreams take flight,
A symphony echoing through the night.

The pulse of the earth, our shared refrain,
A chorus of love in sunshine and rain.
With every beat, with every embrace,
We craft a world, a sacred space.

In moments of stillness, we find our song,
Where vibrant hearts unite, we belong.
Resonating softly, a heart's true call,
Together in music, together we stand tall.

Let the symphony play, let the hearts soar,
Each note a reminder of what we adore.
In the symphony of vibrant hearts,
We find the light that never departs.

The Heat of Resonance

In the stillness, a spark ignites,
A glow that dances, reaching new heights.
Warmth radiates from souls that meet,
In the heat of resonance, feel the beat.

Every glance a whisper, every touch a flame,
Filling the void; we know no shame.
The air is charged, electric and free,
In this fervent pulse, just you and me.

Surging waves of passion cascade,
In the swell of emotion, shadows fade.
Each heartbeat a rhythm, drawing us near,
In the heat of resonance, so crystal clear.

Together we rise, like the sun at dawn,
In this vibrant glow, we are reborn.
With every echo that fills the space,
We embrace this warmth, a sacred grace.

Let the fire burn bright, let the passion soar,
In the heat of resonance, we yearn for more.
Two souls entwined in a glorious dance,
Forever entwined in this sweet romance.

Hidden Patterns of Belonging

In the tapestry of life, threads align,
Woven with care, a design divine.
Patterns emerge from the shadows' play,
In hidden corners, we find our way.

Embers of friendship ignite the night,
In laughter and stories, our hearts take flight.
Unseen connections, a gentle embrace,
In hidden patterns, we find our place.

Through the labyrinth of dreams we roam,
In every heartbeat, we find a home.
Together, we forge a bond so strong,
In hidden patterns, we all belong.

The whispers of time, a soft refrain,
Echoing tenderly through joy and pain.
In every heartbeat, in every song,
We discover the thread where we belong.

Let us celebrate the intricate weave,
The beauty of belonging, the power to believe.
In the hidden patterns that life imparts,
We find our rhythm, the dance of hearts.

Resplendent Regards

In the dawn's soft glow, greetings arise,
A tapestry woven, 'neath vibrant skies.
With every smile, with each tender glance,
We weave our stories, inviting the dance.

Whispers of kindness in every shared word,
Each note of goodwill, beautifully heard.
In laughter's embrace, we find delight,
Resplendent regards, a shimmering light.

Moments of wonder, like petals unfold,
In the warmth of our hearts, a treasure untold.
A symphony of warmth, as souls converge,
In resplendent regards, our spirits emerge.

Through trials and triumphs, we stand side by side,
In the glow of connection, love will abide.
In every exchange, a magic ignites,
Resplendent regards in the still of the nights.

Let gratitude flow like a river of dreams,
In the currents of kindness, we find our gleams.
With every heartbeat, in every embrace,
We share resplendent regards, a sacred space.

Dappled Dreamscapes

Under silver shades we lay,
Whispers of the leaves at play.
Gentle breezes through the trees,
Carrying the scent of ease.

Floating on the clouds of time,
Moments sweet, like hidden rhyme.
Colors blend and softly sway,
In this dream where we can stay.

Sunlight dances on your face,
Every glance a warm embrace.
Laughter echoes through the glade,
In this bliss, we are remade.

Nature paints with strokes so bright,
Casting shadows, chasing light.
Here, in harmony, we tread,
In these dappled paths we're led.

In this space, our souls ignite,
Dreams take wing and soar in flight.
Lost in vision, pure and true,
Dappled dreams, we'll start anew.

Portraits of Us

In the frame of moments past,
We find a love that's meant to last.
Canvas colors blend and swirl,
Every stroke a tale unfurl.

Captured smiles in every hue,
Echoes of the things we do.
Whispered secrets, shared delight,
In this portrait, hearts take flight.

Through the years, we've grown so close,
Each memory a vibrant dose.
Laughter graced beneath the sun,
In these frames, we are as one.

With each glance, a spark ignites,
Painting dreams on starry nights.
Brush of fate draws us along,
In this gallery, we belong.

Portraits of our hearts entwined,
Every heartbeat intertwined.
In the art of love, we trust,
Forever bound, our portraits must.

Chasing Colors

In the dawn, the world awakens,
Every hue in light, it beckons.
Chasing colors, bold and bright,
Through the day and into night.

Fields of gold beneath the sun,
Painted skies, the day begun.
From blue to red, we roam so free,
In this vibrant tapestry.

With each step, we brush the earth,
Finding beauty, endless worth.
Flowers bloom in every shade,
A color dance, in joy displayed.

Chasing rainbows, hand in hand,
Creating dreams that feel so grand.
Every moment filled with grace,
In this world, we find our place.

In a spectrum pure and true,
All my colors start with you.
Together, let's paint our way,
Chasing colors every day.

Reflections in Radiance

In the mirror of the stream,
We catch the light, a fleeting dream.
Ripples dance and shimmer bright,
Reflections whisper with delight.

Every glance reveals the grace,
Of tender moments we embrace.
In the water, truth reflects,
Love's embrace, it never neglects.

Sunlight filters through the leaves,
Telling tales that nature weaves.
Glimmers spark in each soft wave,
In this beauty, hearts are brave.

We are echoes, shining clear,
Reflections drawing us near.
Lost in wonder, hand in hand,
In this radiance, we stand.

Every ripple, every ray,
Guide our journey on the way.
In reflections, find our song,
Radiant souls where we belong.

The Light of Togetherness

In shadows cast by worry's hand,
We find a light, a warmth so grand.
Together strong, we face each storm,
In unity, our spirits warm.

Through laughter shared and gentle tears,
We weave our hopes, dissolve our fears.
A bond that glows in darkest night,
Illuminates the path that's right.

With open hearts, we walk as one,
A tapestry of love begun.
In every hug, in every smile,
We conquer miles, we bridge each aisle.

So let us dance upon this earth,
In every moment, find our worth.
For in this world, though vast it seems,
Together, we can share our dreams.

Rainbow Reverie

A sky adorned with colors bright,
In every hue, a pure delight.
Each arc whispers a tale untold,
Of love and hope, of brave and bold.

The reds, they pulse with passion's fire,
While blues inspire the heart's desire.
Greens like fields where laughter grows,
In yellows, warmth that always flows.

As rain gives way to sunlit gleam,
We chase the magic, live the dream.
With every step on nature's stage,
We paint our lives, page by page.

In this reverie of brilliant light,
The world transforms, takes flight at night.
For in our hearts, the rainbow stays,
A promise of brighter, better days.

Heartfelt Creations

With every touch, a story spun,
Of laughter shared and battles won.
In every craft, our essence glows,
Through love, our passion softly flows.

From clay to paint, our hands unite,
Building dreams in morning light.
A canvas rich with colors bold,
Reflections of our hearts unfold.

In whispered words and gentle grace,
We etch our memories in this space.
A dance of crafts, with hands entwined,
In every piece, our souls aligned.

So let the world bear witness true,
To all the heartfelt things we do.
For in our art, we find our way,
Creating love with each new day.

Colorful Connections

In every face, a story shines,
Like threads of fate and bold designs.
We weave our lives in vibrant hues,
A collage rich with every muse.

From friends to strangers, bonds arise,
In laughter shared, our spirits fly.
A patchwork quilt of joy and pain,
In every heart, a soft refrain.

Through paths that cross, we learn and grow,
In every moment, seeds we sow.
Connections deep as oceans wide,
In colors bright, we stay allied.

So let us thrive in this embrace,
A world transformed, a sacred space.
For in our hearts, we find the thread,
Colorful connections, ever spread.

Radiance of the Heart

In the hush of morning's light,
Warmth arises, pure and bright.
Every beat, a whispered grace,
Painting joy on nature's face.

Love ignites a gentle spark,
Guiding through the shadows dark.
A symphony of tender hues,
Enveloping the skies in blues.

Soulful echoes stir the air,
Reminding us that hope is there.
Together found, in quiet space,
We dance beneath love's warm embrace.

With every pulse, the heart unfolds,
A story of the brave and bold.
In twilight's glow, as stars ignite,
Radiance whispers, pure delight.

Colorful Footprints

Each step we take leaves marks of love,
A vibrant trail, like skies above.
Through fields of dreams and hills of gold,
The stories of our lives unfold.

Painted paths in shades so bright,
Echoing laughter, pure delight.
In every corner, colors play,
Together they light up the way.

From verdant greens to ocean blue,
Each footprint tells a tale so true.
A tapestry woven with care,
In every corner of the air.

In fleeting moments, shadows weave,
A journey taken, hearts believe.
Though time may fade the view we see,
Colorful footprints remain with me.

Layers of Longing

Beneath the surface, feelings flow,
In hidden depths, they softly grow.
Each layer holds a tender sigh,
A story whispered, not to die.

Woven threads of hopes and dreams,
Fragile as the morning beams.
Through every fold, a yearning speaks,
In silence found, the heart it seeks.

A canvas rich in shades of grey,
Where shadows dance and light can play.
Unraveled truth, a song of need,
In every heartbeat, love's true seed.

As layers peel, the soul laid bare,
Within the longing, beauty's glare.
In every breath, we search for light,
In layers thick, a spark ignites.

Emotional Watercolors

A brush dipped deep in feelings bright,
Spreads soft hues in morning light.
Each stroke a memory, rich and clear,
Emotions captured, held so near.

With every wash, the colors blend,
A symphony where hearts ascend.
From vibrant reds to calming blues,
Life's palette holds a world to choose.

Teardrops fall like gentle rain,
Sketching joy and tracing pain.
In every flick, the stories flow,
In water's dance, our truths can grow.

As daylight fades, the canvas glows,
In emotional lines, our journey shows.
Each layer tells of love and strife,
In watercolors, we paint our life.

Artistic Echoes

In shadows cast by dreams alive,
Colors dance and softly dive.
Whispers of the heart take flight,
Crafting art in endless night.

Brushstrokes warm on canvas bare,
Every hue a silent prayer.
Voices mingling, lost and found,
Echoes vibrant, all around.

Textures speaking in the light,
Framed desires, bold and bright.
Each creation tells a tale,
In every stroke, emotions sail.

Glimmers of a past unwound,
In the silence, beauty's found.
Echoed moments, shimmering threads,
In this realm where art once bled.

Life's patchwork laid in fragments near,
Captured laughter, joy, and fear.
Artistic echoes, pure and true,
In every piece, a world anew.

Kisses in Vibrancy

In gardens where the blossoms sigh,
Colors whisper, fluttering high.
Kisses brush the morning dew,
A vibrant palette, fresh and true.

Sunlight spills on petals bright,
Awakening the day with light.
Each hue sings a gentle tune,
Promises made under the moon.

In laughter shared and tender gaze,
Vibrancy weaves through fleeting days.
Hearts entwined in shades of gold,
Stories of love, softly told.

Raindrops fall, a sweet caress,
Their rhythm brings an endless mess.
Painting skies in fiery streaks,
Emotions bloom, the heart still speaks.

Together in this radiant dance,
Each moment bids a sweet romance.
Kisses linger on the breeze,
In vibrant colors, love's reprise.

The Glow of Together

Underneath the starlit skies,
Hand in hand, where laughter lies.
The glow surrounds, both warm and light,
In the silence, hearts take flight.

Promises wrapped in twilight's arms,
Finding solace in each other's charms.
Softly whispering dreams untold,
Two souls woven, brave and bold.

As the day bids its tender farewell,
We find stories only time can tell.
Moments glow in the softest hues,
Together found in the light we choose.

In each heartbeat, a melody sways,
Echoes of love in countless ways.
Light a flame, let it shine bright,
The glow of us in pure delight.

Through the seasons, a dance we'll share,
Creating memories, fine and rare.
The glow of together, forever stays,
A radiant bond that softly plays.

Brushed by Emotion

In gentle strokes, the canvas calls,
Where every heartache fades and falls.
Brushed by emotion's tender hand,
Creating beauty, soft and grand.

Colors blend where memories lie,
An artist's heart, a silent sigh.
Each layer tells a hidden verse,
Of love and longing, joy, and curse.

Cascades of passion, vivid and bright,
In every shadow, a source of light.
Whispers float on the painted breeze,
As time stands still, the soul finds ease.

Brushes dance in rhythmic grace,
Capturing every fleeting face.
Brushed by the dreams we dare to weave,
In this moment, we truly believe.

So here we stand, with brushes in hand,
Emotions flow like grains of sand.
A masterpiece of heart and mind,
In art's embrace, our souls aligned.

Melodies of Togetherness

In the morning light, we sing,
Chasing dreams on gentle wings.
Hand in hand, we walk this road,
With every step, our love bestowed.

Hearts in rhythm, soft and true,
Creating magic, me and you.
With laughter echoing in the air,
Together we conquer, every dare.

Underneath the starlit sky,
Whispers float as moments fly.
In cozy nooks, we find our place,
In every smile, love's sweet embrace.

Every note a sweet caress,
Crafting tales of happiness.
In this song, we blend as one,
A melody that can't be undone.

Vivid Dreams of Us

Through the window, colors burst,
In the dawn, our dreams rehearsed.
Painted skies, in hues of gold,
Stories of us, forever told.

Running wild on fields so green,
In each moment, magic seen.
With every sigh, our hopes ignite,
In our hearts, the future bright.

Whispers shared in secret nights,
In your eyes, the world's delights.
We chase the stars, hand in hand,
Building castles in the sand.

Every heartbeat, a vivid scene,
In this journey, we intervene.
With dreams swirling, bold and free,
Together, we write our story.

Embrace in Watercolors

Dipped in the palette of gentle hue,
Love swirls in strokes, tender and true.
A canvas unfolds in soft embrace,
Each color whispers, revealing grace.

Splashes of joy in the morning light,
Brushes dance freely, painting delight.
Harmony blooms in every blend,
Every drop tells stories, love can send.

Rivers of sapphire, sunsets of gold,
Capturing warmth as the night unfolds.
In each tender shade, hearts intertwine,
Crafting a vision, uniquely divine.

Every stroke speaks of laughter and tears,
Eternal embrace, dissolving our fears.
As watercolors merge, so do we,
In this art of love, forever free.

In the quiet moments, colors collide,
Each brush gives life to love's gentle tide.
A masterpiece painted in shades of bliss,
Wrapped in the warmth of a lingering kiss.

Twirling Through Tones

Let the rhythm guide our feet in flight,
Twirling in tones, lost in the night.
Melodies sparkle like stars above,
Every note echoes the yearning of love.

Around we spin, in shades of embrace,
With every turn, we find our place.
The dance of two, in perfect time,
A harmony weaving through pulse and rhyme.

Whispers of melodies, tender and clear,
Flowing like music, drawing us near.
Holding you close, in a world of our own,
Each spin and sway, love has grown.

Lost in the moment, we twirl and glide,
With hearts intertwined, we take the ride.
Laughter and joy spark in the air,
In twirling tones, we shed every care.

The music fades, but the memory stays,
A gentle reminder of our loving ways.
Twirling through tones, forever we're free,
In the dance of our souls, it's just you and me.

Shades of the Soul

In whispered hues, the soul reveals,
Colors emerge as the heart gently heals.
Blues for the sorrow, yellows for cheer,
In shades of the soul, we see what's dear.

Violet dreams paint the silence bright,
Reflecting the depths, welcoming the light.
Greens of the forest, soothing and pure,
Each tone a reminder that love can endure.

Reds of passion, fierce and bold,
In every shadow, a story unfolds.
Each brushstroke tells of struggles and hope,
In shades of the soul, we learn to cope.

Layers revealing the truth within,
In every color, where life can begin.
Trust in the canvas, let feelings flow,
In the shades of the soul, let your heart show.

Embrace the spectrum, don't be afraid,
In every color, a journey is made.
Together we paint our stories untold,
In shades of the soul, a love to behold.

Light and Shadow of Us

In daylight's glow, we find our way,
The shadows dance where we can't stay.
A gentle touch, the world ignites,
Two hearts entwined on restless nights.

The moonlight whispers secrets shared,
With every heartbeat, love declared.
Yet in the dark, doubts softly creep,
In the silence, truths we keep.

Within the light, our laughter sings,
In shadows fleeting, sorrow clings.
Together here, we face the fears,
In twilight's arms, both joy and tears.

But through the night, we chase the dawn,
Where every shadow, love has drawn.
With guiding stars that touch the soul,
In light and shadow, we are whole.

So let us dance this endless flight,
From shining day to starry night.
In all the places hearts can roam,
Together, love, we make our home.

Fantasies in Bloom

In gardens fair where dreams arise,
Petals whisper softest sighs.
Colors burst with radiant cheer,
In every blossom, magic near.

The fragrance lingers in the breeze,
Painting laughter on the leaves.
In every corner, joy is strewn,
Awakening the heart at noon.

With every bud, a story gleams,
Life unfolds within our dreams.
In secret nooks, the wonders hide,
Where wishes bloom and love can glide.

The sun above with golden hue,
Kisses the world, makes things anew.
With every raindrop, hope reclaims,
The pulse of life within our veins.

So let us wander, hand in hand,
Through landscapes bright, a mystic land.
In fantasies where love can swell,
We find our peace, our wishful spell.

Reflections of Kindness

In silent moments, kindness speaks,
With gentle words, a heart it seeks.
In tired eyes, compassion glows,
A simple act, a love that flows.

The world can change with just a smile,
In every touch, we walk a mile.
For every tear, a hand extends,
In laughter shared, a love that mends.

Behind the masks, we find the truth,
In unguarded strength, the bloom of youth.
The beauty lies in every grace,
In every heart, a sacred place.

So let us nurture every seed,
With kindness sown, we plant the need.
To lift each other through the strife,
In unity, we breathe new life.

For when we shine with hearts so bright,
Together we create the light.
In reflections of the love we share,
The world transforms, a breath of air.

Strokes of Yearning

In quiet nights, the stars express,
The heart's longing for its rest.
Each flicker holds a whispered plea,
In shadows deep, you're here with me.

With every stroke, emotions flow,
In moonlit dreams, we come and go.
Each distance crossed, a bridge we build,
In every silence, love fulfilled.

The canvas vast, our stories blend,
With colors bold that never end.
A yearning wound, a brush that sighs,
In every heart, the love that flies.

So let the strokes of passion rise,
Through every heartache, hope replies.
In every want, a chance to see,
The art we craft, just you and me.

In strokes of yearning, life unfolds,
In hues of hope and tales untold.
The masterpiece, our souls collide,
In every frame, a love abides.

Shades of Serenity

In the quiet hush of dawn,
Gentle breezes sing a tune.
Whispers of the softest hues,
Dancing 'neath the silver moon.

Mountains wear a cloak of mist,
Embraced by a tranquil light.
Streams that murmur secrets low,
Guide the heart to pure delight.

Fields adorned with colors bright,
Swaying in a silent prayer.
Blades of grass in morning's glow,
Cradle dreams beyond compare.

Clouds drift softly, shapes anew,
Casting shadows on the ground.
Each moment a fleeting sigh,
In this peace, we are found.

Nature's canvas, painted clear,
Echoes of a quiet mind.
In every shade, we find the strength,
To leave the chaos behind.

Vivid Memories

Locked away in time's embrace,
Moments dance like flickering flames.
Laughter echoed, soft and bright,
Written down in whispered names.

Sunny afternoons of yore,
Sunlight glistening on the lake.
Breezes carrying stories shared,
In every wave, a memory wake.

Golden halls of gentle dreams,
Looming shadows of the past.
Each face a gem, each smile a spark,
Fleeting joys that forever last.

Holding tight to what we cherish,
A tapestry of love and care.
In the heart, those moments dwell,
Guiding us through every fare.

As photographs begin to fade,
In our minds, the colors thrive.
Vivid memories shape our world,
Keeping cherished moments alive.

Chromatic Emotions

A splash of red ignites the heart,
With passion's fire, it starts to burn.
Yellow shines like morning light,
In happiness, our spirits turn.

Blue waves whisper tales of calm,
A tranquil sea, a soothing balm.
Green fields stretch with hope in bloom,
In nature's arms, we find our room.

Violet dreams of distant skies,
The twilight journeys, deep and wise.
Orange sunsets paint the night,
Fading into softest light.

A canvas filled with human strains,
Each stroke a tale of joy and pain.
In every color, we discern,
The essence of our hearts that yearn.

Together forging vibrant hues,
In every shade, a spark to fuse.
Chromatic emotions blend and flow,
Creating love, allowing growth.

A Tapestry of Us

Woven threads of time and space,
Intertwined in patterns bold.
Stories shared in warm embrace,
Crafting tales that will be told.

In laughter's stitch, we find our thread,
Through tears that weave our bonds so tight.
Each moment a beloved strand,
Binding us in day and night.

Colors blend in harmony,
A tapestry of hopes and dreams.
Every hue, a memory,
Each knot, a promise that redeems.

Underneath the stars we stand,
Admiring what our hands have spun.
A masterpiece of heart and hand,
In every heartbeat, we are one.

Through time's embrace, together strong,
Our fabric rich, it flows and bends.
A living art, where we belong,
A tapestry that never ends.

Palette of Passion

Colors swirl in wild delight,
Crimson dreams that touch the night,
Golden rays of morning's kiss,
Whispers in the air of bliss.

Brushstrokes dance in vibrant tune,
Every shade a love in bloom,
Ocean blues and fiery reds,
In each hue, our story spreads.

Life's canvas broad, emotions bold,
Tales of warmth in glimmers told,
From deep shadows to bright gleams,
We paint our hearts with fervent dreams.

Through every shade, passion speaks,
In silence felt, our spirits seek,
Together woven, bright and deep,
In this palette, love we keep.

The Spectrum of Us

Underneath the endless sky,
Violet whispers, soft and shy,
Emerald hopes that rise and fall,
In each moment, we find it all.

From the dawn in amber light,
To the dusk, a canvas bright,
Every color tells our tale,
In this spectrum, we unveil.

Threads of warmth, a vivid thread,
In the hues, our past is spread,
Together through the swirling grace,
We find harmony in this space.

Every glance a gentle brush,
Every touch ignites a rush,
In the spectrum of our hearts,
Love's true canvas never parts.

Echoes of a Caring Soul

Softly, echoes linger near,
In every laugh, in every tear,
A gentle heart, a tender way,
Reminds us of the light of day.

Whispers shared in quiet tones,
Sheltering soft, forgotten bones,
Every word a soothing balm,
In troubled times, we find our calm.

Starlit skies and moonlit beams,
Where kindness flows like gentle streams,
A caring soul's sweet lullaby,
Cradling hopes that soar and fly.

In the silence, warmth unfolds,
In the echoes, love beholds,
Together woven, strong and whole,
Resonating through each soul.

Hues of Intimacy

In twilight's hush, the colors blend,
Soft lavender and cerulean send,
Gentle warmth, a tender brush,
In stillness found, we feel the rush.

Scarlet whispers, bold caress,
In every silence, hearts compress,
Emerging dreams in closer view,
In every glance, a world anew.

Shadows play, our secrets shared,
In hues of us, we are bared,
Vivid moments held so tight,
In the depths of quiet night.

Each soft glow, a real embrace,
In every shade, I see your face,
Together here, time finds its grace,
In hues of love, a sacred space.

Enchanted Tints of Passion

In twilight glow, our dreams take flight,
Colors swirl, igniting the night.
Brush of love, gentle and free,
Canvas alive, just you and me.

Whispers danced in shadows cast,
Moments captured, forever last.
Crimson skies and sapphire seas,
In your eyes, I find my peace.

Each stroke a promise, a vow so true,
Under the stars, my heart is you.
With every hue, our spirits soar,
United in love, forevermore.

Emerald dreams and golden light,
Painting memories through the night.
Together we weave, a tapestry bright,
In enchanted tints, our love ignite.

Vows in Vivid Pigments

With every color, I pledge my soul,
In vibrant shades, we become whole.
Brushes tremble, hearts intertwine,
In vivid hues, our love will shine.

A symphony of tones, bold and bright,
Creating a dance in the soft moonlight.
Your laughter like strokes on this page,
In vivid pigments, we must engage.

Promises draped in violet skies,
Where love's whispers never die.
Each moment treasured, each heartbeat true,
In vivid pigments, I find you.

With every canvas, our story unfolds,
In colors warm, in colors bold.
Together we'll paint, our lives a song,
In vows of vibrance, where we belong.

Whispers in the Palette

Whispers soft in colors speak,
Each hue a secret, delicate, meek.
The palette sings, a gentle refrain,
In every stroke, our love's sweet gain.

Turquoise tides and amber swirls,
Dancing lightly, our dreams unfurl.
In whispered tones, we find our way,
In the quiet palette of the day.

Shadows linger, colors blend,
In tender whispers, our hearts mend.
With every stroke, our spirits find,
In whispers soft, love intertwined.

Glimmers of gold in soft evening light,
Creating memories, pure and bright.
In the palette's embrace, we'll stay,
Whispers of love will guide our way.

Shades of Affection

In shades of love, our hearts reside,
A spectrum vast, with arms spread wide.
Soft pastels and vibrant flames,
In shades of affection, we call names.

Brushed by time and tender hands,
We paint our dreams on golden sands.
With every shade, a promise made,
In this love, we won't fade.

A canvas rich with laughter's sound,
With hues of joy, our souls are bound.
In every stroke, our futures blend,
In shades of affection, love won't end.

From dusk till dawn, our colors sing,
In every shade, our hearts take wing.
With every heartbeat, every breath,
In shades of affection, we'll find the depth.

Heartfelt Tints

In twilight's glow, soft whispers linger,
A palette of dreams where colors mingle.
Each stroke of love, a symphony sung,
Heartfelt tints of the young and the sprung.

Rainbows dance on puddles of hope,
Beneath the sky, we learn to cope.
The brush of fate paints paths anew,
In every hue, my heart finds you.

Morning breaks with a golden face,
Every petal holds a warm embrace.
In every shade, a story we weave,
Together in colors that never leave.

With sunset's kiss, the world ignites,
A canvas of dreams, bursting with lights.
In the gallery of life we create,
Heartfelt tints we celebrate.

As night descends, the stars arise,
A jeweled sky, where hope never dies.
In every color, my soul finds peace,
Heartfelt tints that never cease.

The Brush of Belonging

Upon a canvas, our dreams take flight,
A tapestry woven through day and night.
The brush of belonging, a gentle hand,
Colors of unity, across the land.

In each stroke true, we find our place,
Hearts intertwined, with tender grace.
Together we rise, in hues that blend,
In the art of living, we find a friend.

Through valleys deep and mountains high,
With every challenge, together we fly.
The palette whispers of love so strong,
With the brush of belonging, we all belong.

Every shade echoes laughter and tears,
With strokes of memories through the years.
In every artwork our spirits thrive,
The brush of belonging keeps dreams alive.

As seasons change, our colors grow,
In vibrant shades, our love will show.
With unity's tone, we boldly sing,
The brush of belonging, our sacred ring.

Melodies in Monochrome

In shadows deep, a tune is spun,
Melodies rise as day is done.
Every note a dance, each silence speaks,
In monochrome dreams, our beauty peaks.

Black and white, a world so clear,
In every heartbeat, love draws near.
Fingers touch keys of passion's song,
In the stillness, we find where we belong.

A symphony plays in the depth of night,
As moonlight bathes the world in light.
Each brush of sound, a lover's embrace,
Melodies linger in perfect grace.

Between the lines, emotions collide,
In monochrome whispers, hearts confide.
A duet of souls, in harmony's flow,
Melodies in tones that softly glow.

In the quiet moments, we hear the call,
Of living in shades, we capture it all.
In monochrome's charm, our spirits will soar,
With melodies sung, forevermore.

Beyond Black and White

In a world of contrast, shadows and light,
We search for colors that feel just right.
Beyond black and white, our spirits roam,
In vibrancy found, we build our home.

Every heartbeat is a brushstroke bold,
Unveiling stories waiting to be told.
With dreams that shimmer in the day's embrace,
We journey together, finding our place.

Through twilight whispers and dawn's warm glow,
We paint our lives in a radiant flow.
Beyond black and white, our journey unfolds,
In colors of courage, our tales are retold.

With every shimmer of hope and despair,
We blend our shades in the open air.
A vibrant dance of hearts intertwined,
Beyond black and white, our love defined.

As stories weave their intricate lace,
In every hue, we find our grace.
Beyond shades of grey, we birth the light,
In our vibrant world, we take delight.

Tints of Togetherness

In the morning light we rise,
Colors bright, painted skies.
Hands entwined, hearts aligned,
In this moment, love we find.

Laughter echoes through the air,
Shared dreams, a bond so rare.
With every whisper, a gentle tease,
Together, we dance with ease.

The sunset glows, a canvas shared,
In every brushstroke, showing we cared.
Side by side, we face the night,
In each other, we find our light.

Through storms and tides, we stand tall,
Together we rise, together we fall.
In the quiet, our hearts speak,
In this love, we find the peak.

As stars adorn the velvet sky,
We weave our dreams, you and I.
In every color, we'll paint our fate,
In tints of togetherness, love awaits.

Vivid Embrace

In a world where colors swirl,
Your smile, my favorite pearl.
With every heartbeat, every sigh,
In your arms, I learn to fly.

With passion's brush, we paint the day,
Vivid hues in bright array.
Every moment feels like art,
Creating magic from the start.

Sunlight fades; the stars ignite,
In our glow, the dark takes flight.
A vivid embrace that warms the soul,
With you, my heart feels whole.

We twirl beneath the silver moon,
In this dance, our spirits tune.
Every glance, a spark, a flare,
In love's vivid embrace, we dare.

As dawn breaks, colors blend and fade,
In this vivid world we've made.
In every brush of soft delight,
Together, we shine in light.

The Art of Heartfelt Harmony

In the quiet of the night,
We find our song, pure and bright.
In whispers soft, we share our dreams,
In heartfelt harmony, love redeems.

The rhythm beats, our hearts unite,
A symphony of pure delight.
With every note, our spirits rise,
In this dance, our love applies.

The world fades as we sway slow,
In gentle whispers, feelings grow.
With every step, we learn to trust,
In the art of love, we adjust.

Brushstrokes paint our evenings warm,
In your embrace, I feel the charm.
Every laugh a tender sigh,
In this harmony, we fly.

As the clarion calls of morning sound,
In rhythm, in love, we are found.
In the art of heartfelt harmony,
Together, we create our symphony.

A Rainbow of Sentiments

Colors vibrant, feelings bold,
In this canvas, love unfolds.
From deep indigo to passionate red,
A rainbow of sentiments, widely spread.

With every hue, a story shared,
In every glance, a moment bared.
With strokes of gold, we paint our fate,
In love's embrace, we celebrate.

Greens of hope, yellows of glee,
In this spectrum, you and me.
A touch of turquoise, calm and true,
In the rainbow, I see us two.

Through every storm, colors may mix,
In each other, we find the fix.
With each brush, we craft and bloom,
In our hearts, a brightened room.

As the sky wears its evening cloak,
In the twilight, we find our spoke.
In a rainbow of sentiments, we soar,
Together forever, we want more.

Brushstrokes of Devotion

In every hue our hearts combine,
With gentle strokes, our spirits align.
A canvas bright, our love's embrace,
Each brushstroke whispers, a sacred space.

Through splashes bold, through subtle grace,
We paint our dreams, no need to chase.
The vibrant shades, in shadows bloom,
In artful whispers, love finds room.

With every layer, stories unfold,
In colors warm, in shades of gold.
The masterpiece of you and I,
Together crafted, we soar high.

Emotions blend, a swirling dance,
Each stroke a promise, a timeless chance.
In galleries of the heart we roam,
In every creation, we find home.

So let our hearts, like colors, bleed,
In every piece, our souls are freed.
Brushstrokes bold, a love so true,
In every canvas, I'll find you.

Chromatic Journeys

Let's journey forth through hues unknown,
In chromatic fields, our love has grown.
With every step, new colors arise,
Reflecting dreams beneath vast skies.

In twilight's glow, we chase the sun,
Two souls entwined, forever one.
Each shade a path we dare to tread,
With vibrant tales, our spirits spread.

Through verdant hills and oceans wide,
In lilac skies, our hearts abide.
With every brush of light and dark,
We light the world with love's sweet spark.

In every corner, colors burst,
Through cloudy days, our hearts will thirst.
In every shade, a journey starts,
With painted dreams, we'll never part.

So here's to paths of colors bright,
To endless days and starry nights.
With laughter shared on colorful roads,
In chromatic journeys, our love unfolds.

The Prism of Passion

In radiant light, our passion glows,
Through prisms bright, true love bestows.
Reflected beams in vibrant dance,
A spectrum born from our sweet chance.

Each color speaks in ardent sighs,
As sunlight floods the evening skies.
In every shade, emotions flow,
In hues of fire, our spirits grow.

With every touch, the world ignites,
In molten hues, our souls take flight.
We paint the stars and call them ours,
In the prism's glow, we find our stars.

Through turbulent storms and calmest seas,
Our passion lives, like gentle breeze.
In every spectrum, love declares,
A radiant bond that always dares.

So let us shine, through night and day,
In colors bold, we find our way.
In the prism of our sweet devotion,
We'll light the world with love's own motion.

Tones of Tenderness

In softest whispers, love unfolds,
In tender tones, our story's told.
With gentle touch and knowing glance,
In subtle hues, our hearts do dance.

Through every tremble, love we find,
In muted shades, our spirits bind.
With silken threads of quiet grace,
In every heartbeat, we embrace.

In twilight's glow, where shadows creep,
Our tones of love, forever steep.
With every glance, a fleeting chance,
In tender moments, our souls prance.

So let us linger, soft and slow,
In whispers shared, our love will grow.
With brushed caresses, sweet and light,
In tones of tenderness, we ignite.

With every note, a melody,
In softest sound, you're here with me.
In gentle echoes, our love stays,
In tones of tenderness, endless days.

Hues of the Heart

In the canvas of twilight, we paint,
Colors of love, bold and quaint.
Whispers of dreams, softly take flight,
Embraced in shadows, glowing bright.

Every hue tells a story deep,
A tapestry woven, memories keep.
Brushstrokes of laughter, splashes of tears,
A timeless masterpiece, through the years.

In shades of passion, we find our way,
Charting the path where our spirits sway.
With every tone, a promise reborn,
In the hues of the heart, love is worn.

From cerulean skies to crimson glow,
Each glance we share, our colors flow.
In the silence, a riot of sound,
In the canvas of love, we are bound.

Together we dance in the fading light,
Wrapped in our colors, hearts taking flight.
A radiant spectrum, fierce and true,
In the hues of the heart, it's me and you.

Radiant Bonds

In the quiet moments, we draw near,
Threads of connection, crystal clear.
A tapestry strong, woven with grace,
In the depths of friendship, we find our place.

With laughter as glue, we cherish the times,
Each memory sparkles, like rhythm and rhymes.
Across the miles, our hearts align,
In radiant bonds, forever entwined.

Through storms and trials, we stand tall,
Each failure a lesson, we rise through it all.
Hand in hand, we silently vow,
In the light of our bond, we always allow.

In autumn's glow and spring's gentle tears,
We share our hopes, we calm all fears.
A friendship so bright, like stars in the dark,
In radiant bonds, igniting a spark.

Through laughter and silence, we celebrate life,
In the depth of our bond, joy conquers strife.
With every heartbeat, our spirits blend,
In the warmth of connection, love knows no end.

Sunsets of Soulmates

As day's light fades, we find our space,
In gentle whispers, we embrace grace.
Golden horizons where we belong,
In sunsets of soulmates, love's sweet song.

With each twilight hue, our hearts ignite,
Burning bright against the fall of night.
In silence, we dream, with hands interlaced,
In the warmth of the moment, time is erased.

The skies bleed colors of orange and pink,
Painting the canvas, making us think.
In the descent of day, we feel so alive,
In sunsets of soulmates, love will thrive.

Sharing soft secrets as stars start to gleam,
In twilight's embrace, we live the dream.
With every sunset, our souls dance free,
In the serene silence, just you and me.

As the world fades away, our spirits soar,
In the magic of twilight, we always want more.
Forever we'll cherish this luminous light,
In sunsets of soulmates, we find our flight.

The Bright Side of Us

In every shadow, a glimmer shines,
A spark of hope in tangled designs.
Through laughter and tears, we find our light,
In the bright side of us, day turns to night.

With every heartbeat, our joy intertwines,
A melody sweet, like flowing wines.
In the simplest moments, we find a thrill,
In the bright side of us, our hearts remain still.

Together we chase the stars from afar,
Finding our path beneath the evening star.
In the embrace of love, we dare to dream,
In the bright side of us, our spirits beam.

With hands held tight, we conquer the fight,
Through the hardest battles, we chase the light.
In the warmth of kindness, we share our trust,
In the bright side of us, we know we must.

So here's to the joy in the simplest things,
To laughter, to love, and the comfort it brings.
In every heartbeat, our souls will trust,
In the bright side of us, it's more than just lust.

The Harmonious Canvas

Strokes of blue and green unite,
Whispers of colors dancing bright.
Echoes of laughter fill the space,
Art in motion, a gentle grace.

Golden sun on a tranquil sea,
Nature's blend, a symphony.
Every hue a tale to tell,
In this world, where dreams do dwell.

Brushes glide with calming ease,
Awakening the heart to peace.
Textures weave a story fine,
In vibrant shades, the soul will shine.

A canvas wide, a heart so free,
Boundless as the endless sea.
Life's palette, rich and wide,
Inviting all to take a ride.

So paint your dreams with colors bold,
Every stroke, a joy untold.
In this dance of light and hue,
A harmonious tale for me and you.

Deep Dives into Color

Diving deep in shades of night,
Emerald hopes, a diamond light.
Cobalt thoughts swim through the flow,
In the depths, true colors show.

Fiery reds and gentle blues,
Each a whisper, soft muse as clues.
Swirling patterns pull us near,
A vivid world, so sincere.

Underwater hues, a calm reprieve,
Where illusions and dreams believe.
Moments captured in fluid spray,
Lost in color, we float away.

Bright oranges spark with delight,
Guiding us through the cool moonlight.
Textures ripple, the pulse of art,
In every color, beats the heart.

To the depths, we plunge and soar,
Embracing shades forevermore.
In the ocean of dreams so bold,
We find our stories, richly told.

Blush of Affection

In soft whispers, love's colors bloom,
Petals unfurl in a gentle room.
Crimson whispers, tender and sweet,
Hearts collide where lovers meet.

Blushing skies at the close of day,
Every glance, a loving sway.
Fingers intertwined, warm and light,
Chasing shadows into the night.

Subtle blush on pale cheeks shine,
In this moment, you are mine.
Each heartbeat painted with desire,
A canvas bright, set hearts on fire.

Tender strokes in a lover's dance,
Unspoken vows in every glance.
Swaying hearts beneath the stars,
In this world, love heals the scars.

So let the blush of love ignite,
Fill the canvas, day and night.
With every color, we shall weave,
A story of love that we believe.

Painted Promises

With every brush, we frame the dawn,
Loyal hearts the canvas drawn.
Promises painted thick and bright,
In the dawn, we chase the light.

Hues of hope on sacred ground,
Every pledge, a vibrant sound.
In the chaos, beauty thrives,
Together, our longing drives.

From the ashes, colors rise,
Artful dreams beneath the skies.
Each stroke whispers, never fear,
In painted promises, we're near.

Every shade a bond so true,
Life's watercolor, me and you.
United, we'll face the storm,
Together, in love's warm form.

So let us paint with strength anew,
In every moment, I choose you.
With colors rich, our spirits soar,
In painted promises, we explore.

The Glow of Affection

In quiet moments, hearts do meet,
A gentle warmth, a soft retreat.
Whispers dance in the fresh night air,
Love's embrace, beyond compare.

With every glance, a spark ignites,
In simple joys, our world delights.
Hand in hand, we face each day,
In the glow, we find our way.

Through trials faced, our bond holds strong,
In laughter's song, we right the wrong.
Together still, we learn and grow,
In the glow of love, our spirits flow.

The stars above, they watch us shine,
In sacred space, our souls align.
Through every storm, we'll brave the night,
For in our hearts, love is the light.

With every moment, memories stay,
In the glow of affection, come what may.
Our journey shared, a sacred trust,
In love we flourish, in us we must.

Colors of the Unseen

Beneath the surface, hues collide,
In shadows deep, where dreams abide.
A tapestry woven of hope and sigh,
Colors of unseen, reaching high.

In whispered tones, the palette sways,
Through silent nights and sunlit days.
Each stroke a story, bright and clear,
The colors dance, they draw us near.

As twilight falls, the shades unite,
In hidden realms, we find our light.
A symphony played on the heart's own strings,
In every shade, love softly sings.

With every glance, the world transforms,
In every heartbeat, new life warms.
The colors blend, they intertwine,
In the unseen, our spirits shine.

Through every moment, wild and free,
We embrace the hues that are meant to be.
In colors vivid, our story's spun,
In the unseen canvas, we are one.

Kaleidoscope of Shared Dreams

In whispered hopes, our visions glow,
A kaleidoscope of dreams, they flow.
Each turn reveals a vibrant scene,
In unity found, we dare to dream.

With every laugh, new patterns form,
In harmony's reach, we find the warm.
A dance of colors, bright and bold,
In shared dreams, our futures unfold.

The fragments spark, igniting light,
In depths of night, they shine so bright.
Through every shift, our stories blend,
In dreams together, we transcend.

With open hearts, we chase the night,
In every vision, pure delight.
A tapestry woven with utmost care,
In the dreams we share, we lay our bare.

Through time and space, our souls unite,
In the kaleidoscope, we take flight.
Together strong, we rise above,
In the dance of dreams, we find our love.

The Soft Radiance of Affection

In tender beams, affection glows,
A soft caress, where calmness flows.
With every touch, warmth fills the air,
In gentle moments, we find our care.

In the quietude, our spirits soar,
In the simple things, we seek for more.
A loving gaze, a shared embrace,
In the soft radiance, we find our place.

Through whispered words, our hearts connect,
In every glance, we both reflect.
The pulse of love, a rhythmic sound,
In affection's glow, we are unbound.

With every dawn, new light awakens,
In every choice, our hearts are shaken.
In passion's warmth, we dare to feel,
In soft radiance, our love is real.

As seasons change and time moves on,
The soft radiance forever drawn.
In every heartbeat, we stand as one,
he glow of affection, our journey's begun.

Threaded with Color

In threads of gold and silver spun,
Life's tapestry begins to run.
Each hue tells tales of joy and pain,
In every twist, love's gentle gain.

Bright reds of passion, deep blues of calm,
We weave our stories, each a balm.
With every stitch, our spirits blend,
Creating patterns that never end.

Through fields of green and skies so wide,
We find our truth where dreams abide.
The vibrant threads unite our soul,
Together, we are beautifully whole.

In shadows cast, or light's embrace,
Each color shines with grace and pace.
From sorrow's hue to joy's delight,
We craft our dreams both day and night.

So here we stand, hand in hand,
In colors bright across the land.
Threaded tight, our fates entwined,
In this grand weave, our hearts aligned.

Cascading Colors of Companionship

Like rivers springing from the earth,
Our friendship bloomed, revealing worth.
Cascades of laughter, joy so pure,
In every moment, hearts endure.

Orange sunsets, minds in flight,
We chase our dreams with sheer delight.
Together scaling mountain highs,
With every fall, our spirits rise.

The canvas bright, our palette wide,
Each stroke a story, side by side.
In vivid hues, we paint our tales,
With laughter's song that never pales.

Through storms that rage and skies that clear,
Our bond, a compass, ever dear.
With every up, and every down,
In every smile, love's golden crown.

So as the sun begins to set,
In twilight's glow, not one regret.
Cascading colors of our days,
In friendship's light, we find our ways.

Mosaics of the Heart

Each piece a tale, a vibrant shard,
In every heart, a mosaic card.
From broken bits to perfect art,
We find our way, a brand new start.

Colors clash, then harmonize,
In the depths of love, each soul flies.
Fragile moments held with care,
Creating bonds beyond compare.

With every laugh and tear we shed,
We build a path, where others dread.
In light and shadow, stories weave,
A masterpiece we both believe.

Though storms may test, and times may change,
Our hearts remain within this range.
No piece too small, no hue too slight,
Together we embrace the light.

Mosaics grow, and so do we,
Each color rich, with history.
In every glance and gentle sway,
Our hearts compose a bright ballet.

The Vibrance Within

A spark ignites, a flame anew,
In shadows cast, we find the view.
With every heartbeat, colors churn,
In vibrant dance, our spirits yearn.

Within the depths, a rainbow swells,
In whispered dreams, where magic dwells.
Emotions flow, a river wild,
In every joy, the heart's own child.

The world may fade, but we remain,
Through radiant joy, or quiet pain.
In laughter shared, in tears unspun,
The vibrance calls, we rise as one.

Beyond the noise, beneath the skin,
A tapestry of light begins.
Through trials faced and battles won,
We flourish bright, like morning sun.

So let us shine, in all we do,
With hearts ablaze, forever true.
The vibrance within, our guiding star,
Together, we can reach so far.

Whispers of the Heart

In shadows deep, where silence dwells,
Soft whispers float, like secret spells.
Tender words within the night,
A gentle breeze, a fleeting flight.

Each heartbeat sings a quiet tune,
Underneath the silver moon.
A language formed in every glance,
A silent call, a sacred dance.

In hidden nooks where lovers stray,
Their souls entwined in sweet ballet.
Among the stars, their dreams take flight,
A tapestry of pure delight.

With every sigh, the world fades away,
In whispered moments, hearts sway.
The secrets shared, a bond so rare,
In the depths of night, all hearts laid bare.

Together they weave a timeless song,
Where every note feels like a throng.
The whispers of the heart will stay,
Forever bright, come what may.

Shades of Affection

In every hue, a story told,
Of love and warmth, of hearts turned bold.
Violet dreams and azure skies,
Each shade reflects the soul's replies.

Amber glows in morning light,
Whispers sweet, the day feels right.
Crimson blushes, tender grace,
In every moment, love finds its place.

Emerald leaves in soft embrace,
Unfold the world with gentle pace.
Golden rays that melt the chill,
A promise of the heart's strong will.

By twilight's gleam, the colors blend,
Each brush of love, a timeless trend.
Dancing shadows on the wall,
In shades of affection, we stand tall.

Through every season, colors thrum,
In harmony, our hearts will drum.
In the spectrum, love will expand,
Painting our lives, hand in hand.

Tapestry of Emotions

Threads of joy weave through the night,
In a tapestry, colors bright.
Soft sorrows sewn with care,
Creating warmth that we all share.

Moments stitched with laughter's thread,
In woven dreams, our spirits fed.
A pattern rich with every tear,
In each design, love draws near.

Textures felt in every touch,
Knit together, holding such.
Warm embraces wrap us tight,
In the fabric of pure delight.

Each heartbeat echoes, gently pressed,
A canvas bearing every quest.
Crafted stories, old and new,
In the tapestry, we find what's true.

Together we stand, side by side,
In this woven world, we confide.
Through every stitch, together we rise,
A tapestry beneath the skies.

The Prism of Devotion

Through the prisms, colors play,
In the light of love's bright ray.
Every angle paints a scene,
In devotion's grasp, we glean.

Reflections dance, a vibrant hue,
In every heart, a love so true.
Crystalline visions, sharp and clear,
In the prism, we hold dear.

With patience, light will bend and swirl,
Creating magic in our world.
A spectrum rich, with every glance,
In the prism, we find romance.

As shadows fall, the colors shift,
A living testament, our gift.
In devotion's light, we see,
A bond forged strong, eternally.

Hand in hand, we chase the beams,
In each glimmer, love redeems.
Through the prism, forever bright,
We paint our dreams in purest light.

The Hue of Hope

In the dawn's gentle light, waiting,
Colors bloom, dreams creating.
Each ray a promise, soft and bright,
Whispers of warmth, banishing night.

Petals unfold, their hues divine,
Crimson and gold, they intertwine.
Nature's palette, vast and true,
A spectrum of life in every view.

Buds of possibility rise,
Amidst the fears, hope defies.
Growing silently in the shade,
A tapestry of dreams is laid.

Morning dew, a glistening tear,
Nurturing love, drying each fear.
With every heartbeat, colors blend,
In the palette of life, we ascend.

In the twilight, hues resonate,
Binding hearts, we celebrate.
Hope's embrace, a tender song,
In its arms, we all belong.

Emblazoned Affection

In every glance, warmth ignites,
Colors dance in soft delights.
Golden threads of sweet embrace,
Woven deep in time and space.

With every whisper, shadows fade,
Brilliance blooms in love's cascade.
Violet skies, a canvas bold,
Stories of affection told.

Passion's fire, an art parade,
Through crimson strokes, our dreams invaid.
Every heartbeat, every sigh,
A rainbow bridge that lifts us high.

Gentle touches, hues collide,
In this world, love shall abide.
Beneath the stars, we'll paint the night,
With colors that feel just right.

Together in this vibrant hue,
Heartfelt shades of me and you.
Emblazoned tales, forever spun,
Two souls merged, forever one.

Echoes of Color

Across the canvas of the sky,
Whispers of past colors fly.
Echoes of joy, pain, and cheer,
Tracing stories far and near.

Each shade a tale of love or loss,
From azure lakes to fields of dross.
In twilight's glow, reflections gleam,
Colorful fragments of a dream.

Fading hues from days gone by,
Painted memories we can't deny.
Crimson tears, laughter's gold,
Fragments of life in shades untold.

Nature's brush, with gentle hand,
Strokes the heart, helps it withstand.
Every moment, a vivid brush,
In silence, the colors rush.

In the echoes, we find our way,
Charting paths where shadows play.
Colors blend as time goes on,
In every heartbeat, we belong.

The Color of Kindred Spirits

In the galaxy of stars so bright,
Kindred souls share the light.
Colors twirl in cosmic dance,
In unison, a shared chance.

Cobalt dreams in night's embrace,
Whispers of hope, a sacred place.
Emerald bonds that tie us tight,
Guiding us through dark to light.

With every glance, warmth awakes,
Harmony blooms, not a mistake.
Rustic shades of deepened trust,
In kindred hearts, we find our must.

Through the storms, we stand as one,
Unified, our journey's begun.
In every battle, colors blend,
The warmth of friendship shall not end.

As time unfolds its vibrant sway,
On this canvas, we'll always play.
The color of spirits intertwined,
A masterpiece, forever enshrined.

Heartstrings in Hues

Tangled threads of vibrant threads,
Whispers dance in colors bold.
Each note strums a gentle chord,
In every hue, our stories told.

Sunset orange, morning's blush,
In twilight's glow, our hearts align.
With every stroke, a tender hush,
We paint the love that's yours and mine.

From emerald greens to sapphire skies,
Our laughter paints the air we share.
In every glance, the meaning lies,
A masterpiece beyond compare.

The canvas stretches, wide and free,
With strokes of passion, fierce and true.
Together we create, you and me,
Heartstrings woven in vibrant hue.

The brush of time will never fade,
Our colors blend, forever bright.
In every tear and every raid,
We find our strength, our guiding light.

The Spectrum of Us

In the prism of our souls,
Colors swirl, they blend and flow.
Unity in every role,
In a spectrum, we both glow.

Side by side through stormy days,
Rainbows leap from depths of pain.
Through the shadows, love always stays,
Chasing after joy, refrain.

Crimson warmth of passion's fire,
Serene blues of tranquil nights.
Each shade reflecting our desire,
In the silence, our love ignites.

Golden moments, fleeting fast,
Shimmer bright in time's embrace.
Memories created, forever cast,
In this spectrum, we find grace.

Together, weaving dreams untold,
In colors deep, we find our way.
A tapestry of hearts so bold,
In the spectrum, we choose to stay.

Emotions Painted Bright

Brush in hand, I start to dream,
Colors splash across the white.
Every stroke, a deeper scheme,
A canvas filled with pure delight.

Joyful yellows, sunny days,
Soft pastels of tender care.
Every color sings and plays,
In each layer, feelings bare.

Cries of red, the passion's fire,
Azure calm, the stillness found.
Gray may whisper, but love won't tire,
In every pigment, joys abound.

Swirling hues, like tides they roll,
Rich purples to the lightest pink.
Together, we create a whole,
In every shade, we always think.

Each emotion, bold and bright,
Paints a story on the breeze.
With each heartbeat, pure delight,
In this canvas, our love frees.

Canvas of Connection

In this canvas, life unfolds,
Every moment brushed with care.
Together, hearts and hands uphold,
A masterpiece beyond compare.

Bold and soft, our colors blend,
From laughter's hues to shadows cast.
In every line, we start and end,
Our love, a bond, forever vast.

With each stroke, our story breathes,
Through painted dreams, our spirits soar.
In darkest nights, hope weaves,
Creating beauty, forevermore.

Brush the fears and doubts away,
Fill the void with vibrant sounds.
Together, we will paint the day,
In every color, love abounds.

The canvas stretches, space divine,
Connecting every heart and soul.
In this art, our lives entwine,
A lasting bond that makes us whole.

Spectrum of Affection

In hues of warmth, our hearts commence,
A palette rich, a sweet pretense.
With every glance, a shade anew,
We paint our love in vibrant view.

Like sunlight kissed by morning dew,
Our laughter blooms in radiance true.
Each whispered word adds depth and grace,
A masterpiece we dare embrace.

Together, we create a space,
Where every moment finds its place.
In colors bright, we dance and weave,
A tapestry of dreams we believe.

Our journey flows in arcs and bends,
With every twist, the canvas mends.
Through storm and shine, our bond holds tight,
In every hue, our hearts ignite.

So here's to love, a spectrum grand,
In every touch, we understand.
A vibrant life, forever shared,
In this sweet art, we are ensnared.

Artful Union

Two hearts entwined, a subtle dance,
With every step, a sweet romance.
Our souls align like brush on slate,
Creating life, we contemplate.

Crafted kisses, soft as silk,
Adorning days like drops of milk.
In every glance, a spark exchanged,
A canvas painted, love arranged.

Together we sketch our dreams so bright,
With whispered hopes that take their flight.
In gentle strokes, our stories blend,
Each chapter rich, it's love we send.

Time flows like paint upon the wall,
In vivid tones, we rise and fall.
An artful union, bold and true,
In every hue, it starts with you.

So let us paint this life we lead,
With every moment, plant a seed.
In colors deep, forever bound,
In this artful love we've found.

Ties that Color

In threads of gold, our lives entwined,
A tapestry of hearts aligned.
With every laugh, a fiber spun,
In vibrant hues, we come undone.

Like petals soft, we intertwine,
With roots that dig, our souls combine.
In days of light, we find our way,
In shadows cast, our love will stay.

These ties we weave, each moment blessed,
With every prayer, our hearts caressed.
Through storms we stand, a sturdy knot,
In colors deep, we share our lot.

With gentle hands, we shape our fate,
In every touch, a bond sedate.
A spectrum rich, our loyalty,
In every shade, our history.

So here's to love, the ties that bind,
In every frame, our hearts aligned.
Through vibrant times and quiet hours,
We grow together, love empowers.

The Glow of Companionship

In twilight's grace, we find our peace,
With every laugh, the worries cease.
A gentle glow that warms the night,
In your embrace, all feels just right.

Through whispered dreams and starlit skies,
In silent moments, love complies.
With fingers laced, we walk the path,
In simple joys, we share the laugh.

Our hearts a compass, guiding true,
With every step, I walk with you.
Together, we find strength to face,
The world outside, our sacred space.

Just like the moon that lights the dark,
You are my solace, my guiding spark.
In every challenge that we meet,
Our bond, a rhythm, steady beat.

So here's to us, a light divine,
In every moment, love will shine.
Through time and change, hand in hand,
Together we will always stand.

The Canvas of Our Souls

In silence we weave, a tale so bright,
Colors of joy, splashed with pure light.
Each moment we share, a stroke so bold,
On this canvas vast, our stories unfold.

Whispers of dreams float through the air,
Textures of hope, painted with care.
With brushes of trust, we define our space,
A masterpiece grown, in love's warm embrace.

Beneath the stars, our spirits will dance,
Every hue whispers, a love-filled romance.
Through shadows and light, our journey flows,
On this canvas of souls, true beauty grows.

Seasons will change, yet we shall remain,
Marking our lives with joy and with pain.
Each layer we add, a deeper reveal,
In colors of heart, our truth is revealed.

Time stands still as we brush away fears,
Creating a world where laughter appears.
Together we stand, through thick and through thin,
In this canvas of souls, it's love that we win.

Twilight of Longing

Dusk drapes softly, a cloak of dreams,
Whispers of wishes dance on moonbeams.
In the twilight glow, shadows entwine,
A longing so deep, for hearts to align.

Stars awaken, with stories untold,
Flickers of hope, in the night's gentle hold.
A sigh in the silence, the world holds its breath,
In the dusk's sweet embrace, we find life and death.

Glistening moments, like dew on the grass,
Each heartbeat echoes, as moments pass.
Beneath the vast sky, our souls reach for more,
Yearning for connection, an open door.

The night stretches on, with dreams yet to weave,
In the twilight of longing, we start to believe.
That love knows no bounds, no distance, no time,
In the shadows we linger, hearts dancing in rhyme.

As dawn breaks the spell, a new journey waits,
In the light of the morn, our love rejuvenates.
Through twilight's soft whisper, hope flickers anew,
In the realm of longing, I find home in you.

Luminous Bonds

In realms of the heart, where kindness prevails,
Connections arise, weaving delicate trails.
Like threads of pure gold, our lives intertwine,
In luminous bonds, our spirits align.

Through laughter and tears, we journey as one,
Shining together, like moon and sun.
With every embrace, our hearts intertwine,
Creating a tapestry, wondrously fine.

Each moment we cherish, a spark in the dark,
As we light up the world, leaving our mark.
In the glow of our bond, true magic unfolds,
In luminous colors, our stories are told.

Through storms and through calm, we stand side by side,
In the warmth of our love, we shall not divide.
Like stars in the night, we shimmer and shine,
In the heart of each other, our destinies twine.

Together we rise, with courage and grace,
Creating a sanctuary, our sacred space.
In the embrace of our hearts, forever we'll be,
Bound by the love that sets our souls free.

Brushstrokes of Desire

With every heartbeat, a vision ignites,
In the canvas of night, passion takes flight.
Brushstrokes of desire, bold and alive,
In the dance of our souls, we find how to thrive.

Crimson and sapphire, a vivid array,
Colors of longing, in the night they play.
Each glance a stroke, each touch a design,
In this art of our hearts, your spirit is mine.

Soft whispers echo through shadows that blend,
A symphony sweet, where desires transcend.
With fingers entwined, we trace out the stars,
Creating a universe, erasing the bars.

The essence of night wraps around our skin,
In layers of passion, we both lose and win.
Each moment a masterpiece, painted with fire,
In the gallery of love, we only aspire.

As dawn peeks through curtains, we hold our breath,
In colors of morning, we find life in death.
With brushstrokes of hope, our hearts will inspire,
In the canvas of love, we burn with desire.